T0124812

A MYTHIC MEMOIR

THE SPRING

Copyright 2021 © Annie Connole

All rights reserved. No part of this publication may be reproduced or transmitted in any form or by any means, electronic or mechanical, including photocopy, recording, or any information storage or retrieval system, without permission in writing from the publisher.

[SOURCE]
Page 85. Pinkola Estes, Clarissa. *Mother Night: Myths, Stories and Teachings for Learning to See in the Dark.* Sounds True, 2009.

[PUBLISHED BY]
Chin Music Press
1501 Pike Place #329
Seattle, WA 98101-1542
www.chinmusicpress.com

First [1] edition
Cover and book design by Dan D Shafer
Cover photograph by Annie Connole
Typefaces: Berthold Akzidenz Grotesk, Adobe Caslon, Tribute
Printed in Canada

[LCCN] 2021935556

[ISBN] 978-1-63405-018-0

THE SPRING

A MYTHIC MEMOIR

ANNIE CONNOLE

CHIN MUSIC
PRESS

For the Animals

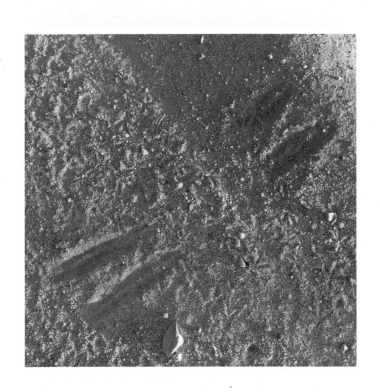

"I also became the river by knowing how it was made."

A River Runs Through It, Norman Maclean

The Spring [DREAM]

The ground begins to shift. I am
standing on a peninsula. Behind me, the
water is choppy and dark. On the other
side, I face still turquoise waters and an
island in the distance. The island is my
destination. A voice says, "Before you
cross, you must tell yourself a fable."

Snake

A campfire glows as the sun begins its descent over a rocky shore of the Upper Missouri River. Flanked on each side by cottonwood trees and lofty white bluffs, the river runs strong and deep.

One of the little boys in our camp is walking to his tent when he spots Snake watching from behind the marsh grass. Snake's rattle twitches like a warning bell. Hearing the boy cry out "Snake!" his father emerges from the tent with a gun. As he looks for Snake, we, a family around the fire, hold our breath. The boy's father steps forward, pointing the gun at the ground.

We know you, Snake. A child sees you. We imagine your tail like a rattle, your smile casting fever dreams into our legs, taking hold, taking us into the underworld, into ancient time where you've lived with the mussel shells since the earth was young. You, Snake, have always been here keeping time, casting your line through the turning of each aeon. We tighten our limbs for fear of madness. We forget our tongues and lose our words. We lose our sight. We imagine clacking and clamoring and surrendering to your spell.

Put the fire light out. Call in the river to take us home.

Deer and Lion

With the fire gone to ash and Snake on my mind, I enter
my tent and sit in the empty space between thin walls.
The painter is usually here, taking off his boots. But today,
he is picking morels in another land.

My ears tune to every rustle in the grass. Snake is out
beyond the cottonwoods, gliding around the rocks. Her
promise keeps me from sleep.

A high-pitched cry erupts, echoing like a symphony in
the wind. It's the cry of Lion, reverberating as a *hiss-
scream*, going toe to toe with Deer.

Wrow! Cccccc. Hissss. Huff. Tear. Mrow!
Huff huff huff. Huff. Wrow! Huff.

Deer, you do not fight. Your *huff* is quiet and determined,
giving, giving, giving and releasing to the sky.

Frog

A few days later, I suggest to the painter that we swap animal stories over dinner.

I tell him of the cat-cry chorus. *I heard the sound of death*, I say. It was like no other. The sky opened.
They let me in.

He tells me the story of Frog. Walking out the door of the mountain house, the painter spotted Frog sitting on the front porch, skin growing taut under the bright, high altitude sun. *How he got there, I don't know*, the painter says. *There is no water for him near the house.*

Seeing Frog was barely able to breathe, the painter took him in his hands and carried him down the hill to the end of the road where a spring bubbled up from the ground. Gently, the painter released Frog into the spring, to be renewed in the waters from which he had come.

Cat and Horse

What would we be if we were farm animals? I ask the
painter as we drive past green pastures on a clear day.

You would be Cat and I would be Horse.
I would watch over you and your kittens.
We would play together and walk side by side.

Cat and Horse, yes, that is what we would be.

Owl

The painter tells me of looking up from the trail along the river road and spotting two baby owls. Through the trees, their unshifting goldenrod eyes cast a long stare into his heart. Two baby Owls. *What does it mean?* he asks. *Two?*

The first time we meet Owl, we are on a hike near the painter's sacred place, White Sulphur Springs. Owl appears like a magician out of the forest, flying overhead with Mouse in its talons. We halt, frozen — Owl's luminous, yellow eyes seizing us. Days later, unable to shake the gaze, we ask our friend what Owl means. *Death,* she says.

The Spring

Days after releasing Frog, the painter jumps into the spring on a full moon night. I never see his face again, except in dreams. He becomes light.

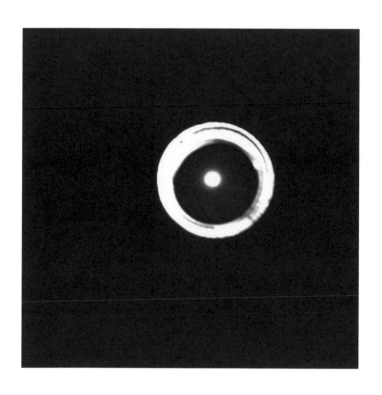

Swan

The light is blinding. I know nothing of the nature of this spring, but it becomes a well in my heart, erupting from my body in tearful heaves.

I fear sleep, because I fear waking one more day to this story.

The painter visits me while I sleep. We sit across from one another at a table. He wears a white long-sleeved t-shirt and his face is covered with white clown greasepaint. *Can't you undo?* I ask. Silent, he stares at me with a deep knowingness, then looks down in remorse and shakes his head, *No.*

So I find two white swans. They are porcelain and fit in the palm of my hand. I buy them to keep us together and place them at the edge of the creek outside the house where I mourn.

Owl [DREAM]

Fires rage in the woods. My mother
and I see a little girl pass by our house.
We do not know her, but the next day I
decide to go out to look for her, afraid
she may have died in the fire. As I begin
to leave, Owl, you tear in through doors
and windows en masse, driving for our
heads. You are everywhere. Owl, you are
taking us.

Black Dog

Old Black Dog, I have never seen such sadness in your body. The weight of this grief is like lead in your bones. Your eyes glisten with tears that cannot come. I ask you, *Does the painter need a friend?* You raise your paw over your face and brush twice over your eye. I ask again, in case it is a fluke. Again, you lift your paw and brush twice.

Tadpole

I imagine the painter is like Tadpole, engaged in a metamorphosis to become Frog. Swimming in hot pools, the only place where I feel light again, I imitate Tadpole becoming Frog. *Swim!* I say in my head to the painter. *Swim. Become.* With all my strength, I push the heavy water behind me. *Become.*

Moose

A couple of weeks before the painter jumped into the spring, he sent an antique picture postcard of majestic Moose to friends in New York. He wrote to congratulate them on their baby, which had not yet been born.

One Sunday, the painter took me to Moose Meadows on the way up Skalkaho Pass. We eased through the gateway of pines to a meadow dotted with cool spring waters where Moose bathed with its young. We did not see Moose, or did we?

Moose, you were elusive. Traveling alone, your mighty shoulders and grand rack of antlers threatened to give you away.

And yet you appear, Moose, on Ceremony Day, when we gather to say prayers for our dead. You appear out of the shadows with the painter's gait, your coat the color of his brown, felted hat. You stroll in front of your old friends, knowing they will see your revival, that they will say your name and tell your story for years to come.

On this day, you walk alone into the clearing where bluestem wildflowers bloom on the mountainside. Just as the ceremony is set to begin, you stride in grace across the road to the chapel, stopping three cars of people who loved you. My grandmother, with whom you laughed and traded stories many nights in the mountain house, makes the sign of the cross as you turn and look her in the eyes while crossing before her, hoof by hoof. Your childhood friends from the city halt in disbelief of you, your shiny brown coat, the perfect velvet fur on your antlers, the way you hold your head high as your eyes meet theirs.

At the altar, loved ones recount the tale of your holy crossing.

Bear

One morning, the painter came home and put on a song by North Bear. He said he heard it on the radio as he was driving into town and began to cry, barely able to see the road through his tears. He found more North Bear songs and we listened to them into the night.

Now, music from the group thunders through the chapel on the mountain.

We saw Bear only once together, at the beginning of a walk into the wilderness, fat on huckleberries, bounding away from us through a field of lupines.

On another day, the painter returned from a long hike to a high mountain lake. He laughed and laughed telling me of the two round ears he spotted near a tree. It was Bear, sitting without a care in the world, watching the wind stir the tall spring grass. When Bear finally rose, their eyes met and the painter glimpsed for a long, terrifying moment the gaping depths of the wild. For nights afterward, Bear haunted him in dreams.

Horse

The painter loved horses. Never has one seen such a
natural rider. He dreamed of having his own horse —
to spoil it with apples, to charm and love it dearly.
He would name it Pie.

At the end of summer, as waterfalls pour through my
cavernous heart, I go out to greet Horse by his stall,
trying to take comfort in his gaze, as the painter
once did.

Tears get in the way of everything.

Dragonfly

I first meet Dragonfly when friends come to see the
places where the painter walked, the mountains he loved,
the sundrenched, high altitude rooms where he made his
paintings. One morning, as we prepare for a drive up to
the chapel, I run outside and there is Dragonfly, sitting
in the car, face pressed against the window, ready to
accompany us on our journey.

Swimming in a hot springs pool, I'm trying to float like
a heavenly body in the clouds. Friends tell me Dragonfly
has been circling my head above the waters all afternoon.

We go to Moose Lake and Dragonfly hovers beside us as
we sit at the shore and talk of our lost friend, of his deep
care for this world. Dragonfly's body is electric blue, just
like the painter's eyes.

I am with my mother at another hot springs. I tell her
about Dragonfly. She asks why she has not seen him.
I say she only has to ask. She does, and moments later,
Dragonfly, big and blue, swoops by us and over the water,
looping around my mother's head.

Sparrow

My friends and I drive to a hallowed place in Yellowstone
called the Lamar Valley. We pause, halted by its openness,
and watch a wolf trot along the riverbank. The bank cuts,
and yet the bank also gives. It makes a hiding place for
the river's doleful song.

We could sit looking across the valley all day. It is so
long, one cannot see the end from the beginning, nor the
beginning from the end. A soft yellow halo hangs over,
infusing each blade of grass with a hushed glow. The aura
is a long breath of clarity amid the fog of grief.

The stars. The stars up there. I haven't seen them yet.
But I imagine each one shedding pale blue light on the
leaves of bunchgrass, on shallow ripples of the river, on
the glassy eyes of the wolf in the dark—just enough to
create a map of stardust leading one to the other in the
slow dance of night.

The slow dance of night takes us.

We want to come back from it.

But it won't let go.

The valley sings me a lullaby, one to release me, like
an old spiritual. My sorrow becomes a chord sung by
Sparrow, words falling from its beak into the river and
pushed heedlessly to the great waters beyond.

Moose

After passing through the Lamar Valley, we stop in
a town at the base of an exalted peak where we eat
fried trout and cherry pie in a log cabin cafe. On the
wall above the kitchen is the head of Moose, mounted
on glossy pine. Moose is dusty, offering daisies, and
radiating a gentle spirit. As we eat, I keep turning my
head to stare at Moose, looking for a sign, a flicker in
the eyes.

We are almost there, I tell my three friends. For years I
have been urging them to visit and take a drive with me
up the tallest peak in Montana. Today is our day.

The young September breeze, moving down through
the dense pines, hovers at the edge of summer's glow
and tells us winter will arrive in the blink of an eye. The
two-lane highway welcomes us back into its faded lines
and we course beside the river, below jagged peaks both
exquisite and merciful.

The road delivers us to the base of the mountain, the one we came to meet. She is the queen of this land and has taken us into her coat of green. We move with her, rising at the edges of steep, verdant slopes, spinning open-mouthed in wonder at the new vistas unfolding with each turn. Crystalline lakes and primordial meadows call to us, ask us to stop for a while. *A picnic?* they say. We nearly surrender, but the mountain urges us on.

Caught in a continuum of new heights, each exceeding the last, we begin to wonder if the bounds of this mountain have no end. We are pushed beyond the clouds, beyond the eagle's ellipse, beyond blue and arrive atop the highest peak in the land.

All is silent except for the roar of wind against my car. We stay inside as I reach into my backpack for a wild plant offering and hold it to a flame. As smoke twirls up from the dried leaves, I say a prayer for the painter. I tell him how much I love him, and that I accept his choice to be born and to die. I bless his life, our love, and his crossing over. The mountain spirits are with us. I turn on the ignition so the smoke will rise through the

sunroof and we are surprised by the abrupt burst of Joni
Mitchell's voice blazing through the speakers,

> *He got the urge for going*
> *And I had to let him go.*

Horse [DREAM]

One night, I find Horse waiting for
me on the other side of the Brooklyn
Bridge. He is a deep chestnut color with
a white star streak between the eyes. I
bring him to my mother's house and
let him graze in a green pasture. Horse
and I have a great affinity towards each
other; we are delighted to be in each
other's keeping. I am protecting Horse
and Horse is protecting me. There is a
lightness and joy between us. I decide
to call him Shadow because the painter
lives on the shadow side — invisible, but
always with me.

Fox

Before snows lock the trail in white, my mother, stepfather and I climb a mountain. After a long ascent, we reach the painter's favorite spring lake — sublime and still, reflecting the mountain's rocky crest like a bowl of holy water.

Poised on pebbles at the water's edge, I reach into a box wrapped in a silk, gold cowboy scarf, and take the painter's ashes into my hand. Pausing over the sky's reflection, I inhale a heavy breath, slowly opening my hand to let the ashes fall. As they float down, they become a constellation of stars, a cosmos reborn at the edge of the spring. Tears spill down my chin and dissolve in the pool, luminous and aglow with the painter's light.

With the sun falling behind us, we silently stride back down the mountain, the rhythm of our heartbeats keeping time with each step.

As we drive through rolling hills, silhouettes of pine disappear into the deep blue of twilight. Fox bursts into the beam of our headlights, an orange streak against the night sky, but disappears before we can ask where he is going.

Wildcat [DREAM]

I walk down a snowy path in the woods
and arrive at a fork in the road. There are
two paths. The one I must take is very
steep. But I am too exposed, too deeply
chilled to go on. Just then, Wildcat
walks out of the forest and graciously
offers me her spotted fur coat. I step
into her legs and my hands become her
forepaws. Her ears and nose flap over
my head like a hat. Disguised and warm
beneath her sheath, I begin making
fresh tracks up the hill through silent,
falling snow.

Fawn

A new year is set to begin with the sun reflecting off a crisp blanket of snow at my grandmother's solitary house. As I step into the light of morning, Deer's family crosses the road to eat beneath a canopy of trees. From behind the most ancient pine, Fawn peers out at me, big ears open to the sounds of ice melting in the morning sun. We watch each other for a long time, breathing white whispers of fortune for the year to come.

Bluebird

My first day in the new desert land—it is December
and I have escaped the minefield of memory up north,
the Christmas carols and the ice. Sand is my snow here.
Patterns can be drawn and washed away instantly by
the wind. The desert wind is strong, cleansing, always
at work, redistributing scraps and bits to distant places,
washing away the hard edges.

I circle the rocks and Joshua trees and creosote bushes
and settle in for a bowl of soup on the patio of a cafeteria
designed by a famous architect. My table sits on a ledge
overlooking hedges and violet flowers. Bluebird appears
and sits on the other side of the table meant for two. I
remain still, my eyes set on Bluebird. Finally, I reach for
my spoon. Bluebird flutters, but does not leave. I dip
my spoon into the soup and Bluebird flaps, rises, and
perches again at the table's edge. As I take each bite, I
never let him leave my sight.

For many meals, for many years, I sat across the table from the painter. Bluebird's royal blue coat is reminiscent of the painter's Mediterranean blue eyes and oxford shirt. Like the painter's majestic eyebrows, Bluebird's thick black eyebrows look as though they have been painted on in two broad strokes. Eyebrows, thick and sleek, were the painter's most notable feature.

As I finish my soup, I reach out to Bluebird. He flutters again, startled, and moves to a branch by my side. Still watching me as I watch him.

Dragonfly

The next day, Dragonfly summons me as I set out in the
sun. Dragonfly loops and lands on the nearest creosote
bush. He shows me his body—rising, landing, moving,
shifting to new branches on the same creosote bush.
I follow the dance, examining his every line and color,
his eyes and wings. Throughout the morning, Dragonfly
does not leave me, so I do not leave him. Finally, I drop
to my knees with tears streaming down my cheeks and
write *GOD* in the sand.

Rabbit

The wind is hushed, and the sun is a dusty rose setting on the deep blue mountains beyond. Rabbit invites me to join its silent world.

Do you not mourn your dead, Rabbit? I held you hours after the flame of your brother died, the baby with the charcoal stripe on his belly. You did not cry or wilt in my hands with grief. You were alive, still in love with the ones beside you, growing new whiskers, ears open to the sounds of life and death.

Rabbit, to be reborn here on the same day was not an accident, so I take you as kin. When I hold you to my cheek, you whisper in my ear like a seashell, telling me of the light places from which you have come. I want to know, because I have forgotten.

Goat

The wind roars wildly across the walls of my desert cabin and I wake to a tap on my left shoulder. The veil is thin. The air is heavy. A presence has entered my house with thunderous gusts. I begin talking to it. Making friends. Asking questions. Giving thanks.

The next day when I go to the neighbor's house to visit Rabbit, I find Baby Goat had been born in the middle of the night. The veil lifted in the thunderous wind so a new one could enter like a bolt of lightning. They are all conspiring — the moon, the sky, the stars, and the spirits to let new ones in. Baby Goat, I hold you to my chest and feel your tiny heart warm mine.

Snake

It is Buddha's birthday, so I offer half an avocado to the stone Buddha sitting in the yard. Turning back into the cabin, I spot Snake climbing up the arm of the wicker chair on the porch. Snake, I don't believe it's you. You must be a stuffed animal. You must be an April Fools' joke.

But no, it is You.

I run inside and take cover by the stove. Clutching my arms, I look up and there is Dragonfly sitting on the paper lantern directly above me. The next day, Dragonfly is dead on the bathroom floor, a delicate corpse lying in a perfect place to be seen.

Bear [DREAM]

I walk through a lush meadow abundant
in blueberries. Bear surprises me, loping
out from behind a bush. Springing
toward me, Bear punctures my neck,
sinking its teeth into my arteries, my
throat. I know I will die. A friend tries
to stop the blood, but I tell her it is
inevitable — this is my end.

Dove

On Easter Sunday, the healers we need appear. Parts of our souls went missing and we cannot go any further without them. The healers know how to bring them back, to make us whole again. They begin a ceremony with us at dusk. White roses. Red roses. Fire. Dove joins my mother and me from her nest overlooking a wooden altar. She watches us as we blow prayers into leaves, releasing all we have been holding onto. The painter's unlived dreams and ours. When the final leaves are laid down, Dove flaps her wings and soars.

Snake

As I examine your paper-thin skin shed beside my house,
you make another appearance. You have arrived, Snake,
covering your old dress with your body, as if to keep it
from revealing your secret. I run back into the house
for my camera. When I return, you have abandoned
your secret to the wind. Rising up the stucco wall and
slithering along my bedroom windowsill, you wag your
tongue brazenly back at me.

Rabbit

During the anniversary week of the painter's death,
I ask for a sign, knowing the days will feel unbearable.
The next day, a big heart appears in the patterns of
Rabbit's fur.

White Alpaca

My breath is low. I go in and out of the sun. In and out
of faith. Slowly, I begin to go underwater again, to the
dark places that have no entrance or exit. As I move
through this thick water, driving around town on a
gravely hot day, I receive a message that a surprise is
waiting for me at the neighbor's place. I drive fast up
the hill, up the mesa, through the washboard sand roads
to my neighbor's corral. Inside the covered stall rests
magical White Alpaca. With long, gorgeous eyelashes,

she blinks over her big glassy black eyes. She sits with her feet tucked beneath her body, wearing a permanent, knowing smile.

White Alpaca appeared without warning—a miracle born to a mother thought infertile. For eleven months, the little one gestated secretly—through the long fall, the winds of winter, the golden spring, arriving in the peak of summer. On the day of her birth, I hold her and we are all lifted. She sits next to me with her head held high toward the sun, as if remembering all the stars of home.

Snake

Snake, your dress has blown from the crevices between rocks with the great winds of August. I take your papery skin, soak it and clean all the dirt away so that it becomes translucent — a gorgeous ivory slip.

Dragonfly

During a trip to New York, where I once lived with the painter, I saw him everywhere in the city, in all the thin boys who strolled through the park ahead of me. Back at the cabin, my troubles feel like they have been exhumed from my body. There is space for light again.

I find you, Dragonfly, with another, a pair of you frozen in time. One inside and one outside. One at the door and one at the window. Were you trying, perhaps, to reach each other?

Wolf

I go north for a winter visit to Yellowstone to hear the lullaby of the Lamar Valley under a blanket of snow.

Yellowstone is where rivers begin and alight. A primordial landscape. A hunting ground for many.

Near dusk, Wolf, you begin a winter evening hunt. As my car rolls up beside you, I fumble to grab my camera, but you look away, resisting my lens.

Carefully, you make your way through the elk and buffalo tracks. Determined, I lean through my window and make a picture of your flawless silhouette against a blank canvas of white snow. Tail pointing east, eyes gazing west.

From this stillness, you leap into your hunt. Jumping through hoof prints, you track a scent for minutes that feel like hours. I get out of the car so I can watch you dance along the trail.

At one point, you pick up a mouse and carry it briefly before dropping it. Was it rotten? Perhaps frozen? You go on making time, leaping and bounding, keeping your nose close to the ground. In this small window of the hour, you have covered a vast swath of land.

Wolf. Despised and outlawed, you are the finest hunter of the forest.

Deftly tracking, I watch you pause, leap, pounce, and dive into a field of white. Come up empty.

Scents hide, scatter, confuse. They disperse, then return with ferocity, moving straight to the gut, the head, the heart, the hands, all over. Shake me up. Feel like stars in my veins. Bang around until it feels like I might pop.

Wolf, have you ever carved a heart out?

I move through new and old tracks of Yellowstone. Many happy returns. But on this trip, I am alone, hunting ghosts, hunting things I cannot name, hunting elusive silhouettes with a steady knock on the inside of my heart drumming a low beat.

The scent becomes muddy. A heavy heart threatens to slow me down. The weight of love's memory. The heart could rupture, give me away.

I think of ley lines—telluric pathways, magnetic energy currents flowing around the earth. They can become routes, highways of information that lead us through invisible trails of the universe. I hear they can help us arrive at our uncharted destinations.

Wolf, I watch you stab at something, both paws suspended, diving down with exposed teeth. But just as your nose brushes over fur, your prey disappears.

Ley lines. A string of light surrounding the earth. Some say this is how geese return to the same spring each year.

Can you feel it, Wolf, that strong pull? Or is it a push?

Lone Wolf

That night, I go to the pool bar at the old hot springs
hotel, have a beer and try to talk to some guys sitting
next to me. The scent isn't there, but I want it to be, so
I stay a while and hope the music will get better, that it
will become real jukebox music, the kind that makes you
sway and lean into the one next to you for a kiss. But this
is one of the new digital jukeboxes, the kind that display
their wares on a blinking neon screen. I want the kind
of jukebox where you can hear the clicking of the album
jackets flipping from side to side, turning the browning
edges of playlists over and over to your delight. I want
the kind of jukebox that will help me remember that
thing, that thing that left my heart, remember the scent
I'm supposed to be following.

So, I go out to the pool and swim to the deep end
beneath the winking moon and stars, no longer believing
they will guide me, but still intimidated by their potency.
The painter was taken on a full moon night. What else

can they do? By tracking the tail of desire, listening to ley lines, I resist a fate divined by stars.

Where are you, Wolf? Did you catch it?

They often call you *lone* wolf, but really you are alone only while hunting. When night comes, you circle up with your pack. And yet, sometimes, even when you're with them — rolling around, playing, caressing, jostling, sparring — you are still alone in your heart.

Buffalo

Sitting at the edge of the Gardiner River, I hear the
sound of Buffalo breathing and watch the herd as their
breath becomes one with steam rising from an ache of
the ground. They graze on the bank, slowly chewing their
cud, and doze into heavy-lidded dreams.

Winter air is easy on the skin today. No wind, only a deep calm from the waning glow of the golden sun and immutable roar of the river rushing by. The ice is at the edge of its melting point, fading to reveal the bluestem grass of fall. Buffalo works a nose into the ground, digging up new bunches of leaves between billows of snow. I gaze at the evening sun calling from behind the mountains, casting long shadows over the silver river.

Buffalo are the gatekeepers of the Park, distracting us from the stirrings of other animals. Guardians of invisible thresholds, they stand between worlds. Big and steady, they keep our eyes from the white-tailed jackrabbit, the lynx, or the mountain goat making its way along the craggy edges of yellow cliffs against a muted sky.

Later, as I drive alongside a herd of Buffalo running up a steep mountainside beyond Soda Springs, I become uneasy. My power pales against theirs. I want to get out of my car, let it vanish as I cross the threshold and run too. I want them to lead me to the place where they will rest, let me lay down beside them, show me where the otters swim in warm pools and the trumpeter swans lay their eggs.

Owl

I return to my cabin in the desert and find a photo in an old magazine of Owl flapping its great, grey wings in a river, feet and underbelly submerged, swimming upstream. Owl is not looking back. This is what I see, because I too am swimming upstream. Fish out of water, owl out of sky. Some days are for swimming. The river takes the shape of a snake, winding a path certain and strong.

Drops of water spin off each wing as they almost take flight, but then dip down again, always pushing, pushing against a heavy current.

Myths slow me down. They are the upstream current of the river I choose to swim. A myth of flying. Of staying in flight. Becomes a story of falling, surrendering to water.

Bluebird

As I am out hanging up clothes to dry in the desert sun,
one of my neighbors, a tiny, elderly woman who feeds
the coyotes, calls to me.

Shrike is back, she yells from across the road.

Looking out from the clothesline I ask, *What is a shrike?*
I walk over to hear her more clearly.

*Look it up — shrike. I put turkey out for him on that blue
post and he returned. He brought a new family.*

How long has he been gone? I ask.

She leans on her chain link fence. *I hadn't seen him since
last year when he got in a fight with a blue jay — no, a crow.
Knockdown drag-out fight.*

What do you think the fight was about? I ask.

*Territory, I suppose. He used to come every day for his turkey.
Ground turkey, like I feed to the roadrunners.*

She pauses for a moment, then says, *I almost finished painting the statue of him.* She goes inside and brings out a plastic patio decoration, in which a bird is perched over a small water basin.

I didn't get to the blue yet, she says. *See, I painted the black over the eyes.*

Looking at the statue, I realize I *do* know Shrike. It was a blue shrike that sat across from me on the patio as I ate lunch my first day in the desert. I called it Bluebird.

A few days later, she rings the door of my house.

Did you look it up? she asks.

What?

Shrike.

Yes, I have seen Shrike. I think it's a sign my late partner has been reborn.

Snake

Snake, you come out of your den and sit beneath the
lawn chair a few feet from my back door. We stare at
each other. My green eyes meet your beady black ones.
Your dark tongue reaches out to taste the molecules in
the air.

When I move, you move. You transfer energy to me.
An unbreakable circuit forms between our eyes. My head,
my neck, my arms, my ribs become light and I feel as
though I may fall over. But I stay with you, transfixed,
exchanging energy, vision.

You speak in your own language — one I know in the
deepest part of my breath, in the serpentine sigh of my
own body.

Owl

I come across a strange mark, an imprint in the sand. The mark is at least a foot in diameter with the impressions of a body, head and wings. I'd never seen such an uncanny print and wonder if I should believe in the materiality of angels.

My neighbor says, *It was probably the owl that sits on the telephone pole keeping watch over your house at night. They take baths in the sand. In Arkansas, we call them sand angels.*

I laugh, imagining Owl plopping down in the middle of my yard making sand angels outside the window where Snake hunts her prey and my spirit roams at night.

Snake

This is how I remember you, Snake. Your brilliant green scales drape like an evening gown and your eyes shine like obsidian, reflecting my image back to me. You twist and rise so high that your gaze meets mine on the horizontal plane. White light emanates from your body, forming a radiant halo. Your mouth is pink and flung open with a ferocious desire to speak. Speak!

Owl

One evening as I sit at my window staring at the night sky, I am startled by a voice booming forth out of nowhere through my room. My breath stops. I look around. Nothing moves. After a few moments, I realize the voice is coming from an audio program I tried to listen to earlier in the day: *Mother Night: Myths, Stories, and Teachings for Learning to See in the Dark*. Now, all these hours later, the book auspiciously begins at this passage, filling the empty space of my room:

> *In ancient mythology the owl was considered the helpmate of many gods and goddesses because it could fly during a time, it could move during a time when most others could not see their way clear. So, the owl comes to mean the ability to see into, to see under, to see around. And to fly with sureness and agility through storms, through lightning strikes, through the dark, and to arrive whole, safely and with mission either in hand or completed.*

Alpaca

Tia, the yearling alpaca, sits by the communal water dish, bearing out the hottest days of summer. Guarding the reservoir for the baby in her belly, she rests in a *cushed* position—knees bent on the ground and head poised—perfectly level with the water. At dusk, she chooses a fresh bed to gestate a new life on her own.

Deer

One July morning, I begin to consider leaving the solace of my desert home. As I'm pouring coffee, a neighbor calls, asking to come over. There is an urgency in her voice. She wants to tell me something in person. Within minutes, she is sitting on my couch, describing a dream she had the night before:

> *I don't know if this will mean anything to you, but I had the sense I needed to tell you about my dream. I was in a meadow. A deer was sitting still in the grass. A glass case covered the deer. And then I saw a handle attached to the back of the deer. And then the deer was pulled out from beneath the glass case. There was an immense sense of relief. But the deer was not me, the relief was not mine. I knew it was yours.*

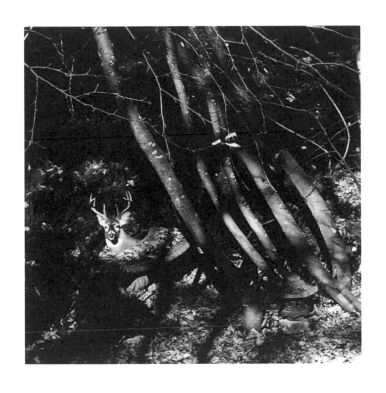

Snake [DREAM]

I find you, Snake, sculpted into a glass
necklace for sale in a museum store.
You have long fangs and apple green
eyes. I take you, put you on, and let you
speak from the fathomless place at the
center of my chest.

Deer

I decide to look for a new home beyond the desert. Friends let me stay at their house while I search. The first morning of my hunt, Baby Deer is found sleeping beneath an old pine beside the window of the room where I sleep.

Horse

Rabbit and I drive in circles, through busy streets,
looking for a new home. After weeks, I almost give up.
But finally, a house calls out to us. The landlady tells me
I'll pick oranges from her tree and Rabbit will bound
through grass in her yard. *Oh, and there is a horse that
lives in the neighbor's backyard,* she says. *You will hear
him neighing over the fence.*

Alpaca

When I return to the desert to pack and say goodbye, I learn that Alpaca will be moving too. So I visit the herd, now seven with one on the way. Walking with them at dusk, I cheer and laugh as they play games in the sand.

One evening, as I watch Rabbit play in the yard, I receive a message from the neighbor: *Tia had her baby*.

Only a ribbon of yellow is left aglow above the mountains in the September sky. I run down the road and find Tia's baby with damp red fur trying to stand on spindly legs. After pausing in awe, I taker her into my embrace. A long swan neck curls against my chest. Her eyes become heavy as her head finds a resting spot on my shoulder. I put my nose to the scent of her sweet newborn fur and feel her hollow bones breathing.

A dream from the night before returns — the painter disappears when I tell him I'm moving out on my own. His stark absence in the dream haunts me through the day, but it's punctured by the wet nose of the baby, the certainty of her newly born body rising and falling with breath in my arms. We rest there a long time, letting the black sky fall all around us.

Back in my yard, I reach through the dark to bring in Rabbit's gate, but my hand lands on a rock in the sand. I bring it inside to examine under the light. The rock makes the clear shape of a heart.

Dragonfly

Friends arrive to conduct closing ceremonies. We are talking in the living room when one goes to the window and exclaims, "Dragonflies!" Outside, five prodigious Dragonflies circle over the garden. They fly among us. They soar in celebratory swoops over our heads, making figure eights until dusk, as if orchestrating a song that pronounces the end of a grand opera.

The following day, I wake in the middle of the night and turn on my bedside light. It illuminates blue Dragonfly, perched on the lamppost. I smile and sigh, knowing he knows it is almost time for me to leave.

Alpaca

A few nights later, I return to see Tia's baby. A somber mood looms over the yard. The neighbor comes to the gate and opens it slowly.

The baby died, he tells me. *I found her this morning laying on her side. I don't know what happened, she was milking the night before.*

We walk out to the backyard. Tia approaches me, then walks away toward the baby's grave marked by a brick in the sand and makes a low call. The other alpacas gather around.

She's still calling for her, the neighbor says.

A few days later, as I drive away with most of my belongings on a moving truck, the alpacas are taken away in a trailer. When I return to say my final good-bye to the neighbors, I ask about the alpacas and how they fared on the trip.

Everyone did well, except Tia, the neighbor said. *She fought me. She clung to me. She wailed the whole way. She didn't want to leave her baby.*

The Spring

One snowy afternoon, as the sun keeled toward the
horizon, the painter and I took a trip to the Boiling
River of Yellowstone. Along the edge of the icy riverbank,
a small fence designated our entry point. It was dangerous
to walk down a river trail at dusk. Rocks and tree roots
waited to trip me up. But the painter held my hand,
making sure I'd know if there was ice, a stump, a quick
turn from the ledge. He signaled when we reached
the end.

We tossed our coats, hats and mittens beneath a bench
and dashed to the river's rocky edge. Steam rose from
the surface where a hot spring geyser merged with the
current of snow run-off. We tiptoed over pebbles and
with cold wind at our backs and lowered ourselves into
the pooling water.

If you get too close to the source, you will burn.

If you get too far from the source, you will freeze.

Death winks at every turn.

But if you find the sweet spot and surrender where the icy flows mingle with boiling water, you will be set free.

Crests of baptismal spring poured over our shoulders, tugged at our feet, and threatened to take us along. Each exhale formed its own mystery.

The body begins to know itself as water.

Old skin dissolves.

Let it go.

And rise from the mist in a new one.

Snake [DREAM]

I have brought you, Snake, to an island
that is a wooden deck in an endless sea
of tilled dirt. People surround us and I
want to show you off, to awe them. But
you pay no attention. Your head rises
from a coil. Levitating, your bright
green body moves from side to side
cutting through the air. You reach the
edge and dive in.

Deep into the soil you swim, carving
new channels through the land, at home
in the rich world below.

Acknowledgements

First, thank you to my loving parents Neil Connole and Joan Leik, as well as my stepfather, Jeff Lepley.

Thanks to the publisher, Bruce Rutledge; the editor and shepherd of this book, Todd Shimoda; and everyone at Chin Music Press, including Shin Yu Pai and Dan Shafer.

Many thanks to those who offered editing, advising and advocacy for this book along the way, including Deanne Stillman, David Ulin, Brooke Swaney, Tod Goldberg and my agent, Dara Hyde.

Thank you to the Golden Dome School, Writing into the Abyss Angels and to all of my teachers and the writing community at the University of California, Riverside Palm Desert MFA program. Thank you, Prageeta Sharma.

Much gratitude to the friends and family who were in some way present for the animal communions in this book, including (but not only) the late Devin Leonardi, Marah Connole, Kathleen Leik, Linda Danforth, Tom and Donna Leik, The Koon Family, Kitte Robins, Maura Kane, The Sutter Family, Brooke Swaney, Meghan Harrington, Hannah Davis, Joe Binder, Jessica Gorman, Kolby Yarnell, Brian Kahn, Electra Stafford, Natalia Molina, Kendall Morgan, Paul Nussbaum, Lisa Nussbaum, Eefje Theeuwes and my neighbors in Joshua Tree.

A deep wellspring of gratitude to the animals, the dreamworld, the land, and the caretakers of the land upon which this story unfolded.

Natalia Molina Photography

[AUTHOR]

Annie Connole is a writer living in the Mojave Desert. She was born and raised in the rocky highlands of Helena, Montana. Annie received a BA from The New School where she studied art and philosophy and an MFA in Creative Writing from University of California Riverside—Palm Desert. Her work has appeared in literary journals including *The Rumpus*.